First published in Great Britain 1994   ISBN 1
Revised edition published 2001   ISBN 1

G000041583

THE LIVING Huɔ ı ∪ʀ ı

OF OUR

HEDGEROWS

Copyright © Lesley Chapman 2001
Illustrations by Brian Steffens

Orchard Publications
2 Orchard Close, Chudleigh, Devon TQ13 0LR
Telephone 01626 852714

Typeset and printed by
Hedgerow Print
Crediton, Devon EX17 1ES

CONTENTS

Centre Page Pull-out (not numbered)

THE LIVING HISTORY OUR HEDGEROWS

INTRODUCTION

Hedges are disappearing from our countryside at an alarming rate. Environmentalists campaign, quite rightly, about the loss of such incredibly rich habitat and its importance to the birds, animals, insects and plants which thrive in hedgerows. To add weight to their campaign, as well as for its own sake, this book has been written to attempt to show how important hedges can be to the historian or archaeologist, whether they be professional or members of the public who are interested in the countryside and its peoples in the past.

Landscape archaeology is a relatively new area of study and began with a work entitled *The Making of the English Landscape* by the late Professor W.G. Hoskins, in 1955. Professor Max Hooper, during the mid 1960s, first realised that the oldest hedges had most species and worked out a formula for dating them by counting the different species over a given distance. It is their pioneer work which led to the current interest in hedges as historical records.

The dating of hedgerows is a fascinating study which requires no equipment and in which absolutely anyone, including children, can participate. It is hoped that this work will help to encourage people to take an interest in hedgerows, realise their importance as historical records, and aid the fight to preserve as many as possible from destruction.

THE FIRST HEDGES

The first people who lived in Britain were not farmers; they lived by hunting, fishing and gathering wild food in the forests that then covered this country. Farming spread here from Europe about 6,000 years ago, and the great forests began to be cleared for farmland. Fields were created and these needed boundaries. A hedge, wall or fence gave protection from large wild animals and kept the farm animals in, as well as acting as a wind-break to protect the crops.

These borders also marked out the exact territory owned by the farmer, and very often larger boundary hedges, fences or walls were built to mark out the tribal boundary, and were used for defence against other tribes. Walls however, require an available source of stone, are labour intensive to build and require continued maintenance. Hedges were therefore preferred, as they were easily built, although a fence may also be required for a few years until the hedge is thick enough to be stock-proof. Hedges are also extremely useful to man when they are grown.

Because the early farmers did not have large ploughs, they had small, easily-managed fields. The earliest fields which still survive date to the Bronze Age which lasted from about 2,000 to 1,000 B.C. They can be seen mainly in Cornwall and in the highland areas of Britain where they are usually surrounded with stone walls rather than hedgerows. Elsewhere, in lowland areas, the soil was better and later farmers with bigger ploughs changed the shape of the fields. The Romans, for example, built fields with straight borders and the Saxons had fields that were long and thin, often with curved sides because their ox teams needed a large turning circle.

The first conclusions about the date of a hedge can therefore be made from the shape of the fields they enclose. This cannot, obviously, apply to individual fields in isolation, but the pattern of the fields when seen together.

EARLY FIELD SHAPES

BRONZE AGE FIELDS

Small, round or sub-rectangular with no sharp corners, they survive mainly in Cornwall and the highland areas of Britain. Recent work has shown that not only the field boundaries but also tribal or territorial borders were marked with borders or hedges.

ROMAN FIELDS

These are square fields, each side being one stadia long, the Roman unit of measurement. These have been found in East Anglia, Sussex and Gloucester. Work is continuing but there is still much to be done in other areas.

MEDIEVAL FIELDS

The first historical reference to a hedge in this country is recorded in the Anglo-Saxon Chronicles in the year 547 A.D. During the seventh century laws were passed stating that it was the responsibility of the farmer to ensure that the hedge or fence around his fields was stock-proof. If any stock got in and damaged his crops no compensation would be paid.

The oxen teams needed a large turning circle, hence long, thin reversed S shaped fields.

Many Saxon place-names derive from the word for hedge. Hay, Hayes, Hayne and Hey are all parts of place-names which mean 'enclosed by hedges' and are very common in England. The oxen teams which pulled the Saxon ploughs needed a very wide turning circle. As they always turn anti-clockwise in the northern hemisphere, the result is a reversed 'S' shape to the long and thin fields.

Later, in the Middle Ages many people living in villages developed a way of sharing out the land in a way that was fair to everybody. They divided the land round the village into two or three big fields. These were then divided into strips, all twenty-two yards wide and two hundred and twenty yards or one furlong long. (Many of these old measurements still survive today. A cricket pitch is twenty-two yards long, and some horse races are still measured in furlongs.) Everybody in the village had strips in the good soil and some strips in the bad soil. Dividing the strips was a low grassy bank or mound, where goats may have been tied to graze. This kept the grass short on these mounds and prevented a hedge growing. This arrangement left a striped pattern on the ground known as 'ridge and furrow' and can be seen all over the country, but most clearly in the Midlands.

The lord of the village or manor had most strips, and all the villagers had to work on these strips for him. When a farmer had earned enough money to buy more strips, he would normally plant a hedge round his part of the field. This hedge was usually planted with hawthorn (the name means 'hedge-thorn' and is a Saxon word) with an oak tree planted every twenty-two yards, that is, at the end of the old strips. This process of increased private ownership led to the disappearance of most strip farmed fields.

The exceptions are at Laxton in Leicestershire and Braunton in Devon, although remnants of these fields can be discerned all over the country by measuring the lengths of the hedges, which are in multiples of twenty-two yards, and by looking for oaks in hedgerows also spaced every twenty-two yards.

Written evidence of hedges can assist with dating. In the Saxon period, many lands or estates were granted by charters. These charters were written and stored in the churches for safe keeping. They were written in Latin, and gave all the boundaries in Anglo-Saxon, so that everyone could understand where they were. Many of these boundaries can be traced on the ground today, and the hedgerows along them, often mentioned in the charters, can be said to date from at least that time. They may of course be even older, as the Saxons donated parcels of land that may have already been estates dating back to the Romans, or even earlier. Boundaries of land tend to remain intact even after conquest. Much work is currently being done on the antiquity of estates of land, but it has been noticed that four fifths of the Saxon estate boundaries now form our parish boundaries.

DATING OF HEDGEROWS

In Devon there are many Saxon charters, the earliest dating to 739 AD. It was by using some of these charters that Professor Hooper was able to test his formula. The formula was based on studies of hedgerow species in over two hundred and thirty hedges from East Anglia, the East Midlands and Devon. Technically it is:

That in a thirty yard stretch of hedge the age of hedge = (number of species x 110) + 30 years. But there is a much easier formula:

THERE IS ONE NEW SPECIES IN A HEDGE EVERY HUNDRED YEARS MEASURED OVER A 30 METRE LENGTH.

To date a hedge by this method, it is necessary to measure or pace out a length of thirty metres, then count the number of different species of TREES and SHRUBS in that length. These are recorded on a worksheet and another thirty metres paced out until either the whole length of the hedge is recorded, or six counts have been made and an average number for the hedge can be worked out. It is best to avoid the end of hedges, gate entrances or where there is woodland adjacent to the hedge.

The commonest species are listed and drawn later in this book for identification purposes. It is best to date a hedge in summer but it can be done in winter providing you are familiar with varieties of twigs. Some trees are indicators of an old hedge, because they will only grow when the hedge is thick enough to shelter their very delicate saplings. Dogwood and Field Maple will only grow if there are already at least four species well established, so if you see either of these two trees in a hedge you can conclude it is over four hundred years old at least. Spindle needs an even thicker hedge for its seedlings, so a hedge will have to be six hundred years old before Spindle occurs. Hazel is a sign that the hedge is ancient as is the presence of the three flowering plants: Dogs Mercury, Bluebells and Yellow Archangel.

The dominant species in a hedge can give clues to the age as follows:–

1. Hawthorn: Hawthorn dominant is probably a fairly new hedge, not yet colonised by other species. An unintentional hedge is also likely to be hawthorn, because of the speed it grows and it is not likely to be eaten by animals, because of the thorns.
2. Hazel is an indicator of former woodland, and of great age of the hedge.
3. Ash was deliberately planted for tool handles, so if this is dominant, it indicates a deliberately planted hedge.
4. Beech and Sycamore were popular in the eighteenth century, and deliberately planted for their appearance.

In order to date hedgerows it is essential to have a map of some kind so that the exact hedge can be recorded. The Ordnance Survey 1:25,000 series (2½ inches to one mile) shows the field boundaries, as well as parish boundaries and is simple to use for hedge dating. For looking at a small area in great detail, the Ordnance Survey six inch map is ideal.

The Tithe Map series of 1840, available from your local Records Office, are particularly interesting as they also show the old field names which can also be clues to dating hedges.

It was by studying a Tithe Map dating from about 1840 that remnants of strip fields were found in the parish of Sampford Courtenay in Devon, a county where strip farming is commonly believed not to have occurred, apart from the Great Field at Braunton. These fields were called Alderland (Old Land) and a count of the woody species around the remains of these fields showed the main hedgerows dated to about the time of the Norman Conquest, nine hundred years ago, with a consistent nine species. The intervening hedges had only four or five species. These figures were exactly the same as the figures I obtained from hedges at Braunton Down, where there were, according to the Tithe Map, strip fields like the Great Field. (The Great Field itself is so close to the sea it only has three or four hardy species.)

This would make the history of strip farming in Devon something like this:— About the time of the Conquest, the fields were laid out in open fields with individual strips. This was the time when children were employed to look after animals in unfenced lands, the 'Little Boy Blue' and 'Little Bo Peep' of the nursery rhymes. There was a large increase in population in the Middle Ages in Europe, so farming methods to provide food for this increased population had to change. The fields were farmed in strips for five or six hundred years. Then during the sixteenth century the peasants became more prosperous and were able to buy their freedom. This was a result of the manpower shortage following the Black Death in the fourteenth century. These free men then planted hedges round the little areas of land they had managed to acquire, giving rise to the field shapes shown in the diagram on page 10.

From 1400 to 1600 Enclosure Acts were passed, and common land was divided into fields, enclosed by new hedges. These laws stopped in Cromwell's time and some regulations were made against the enclosure of common lands, but from later in the seventeenth century there was a great planting of hedges because of new Enclosure laws. Many commons and moors around the villages became fields, instead of wide open places where all the villagers were free to graze their animals. These enclosure fields tended to have long, straight hedges, enclosing big square fields. It is estimated that half of the fields in England

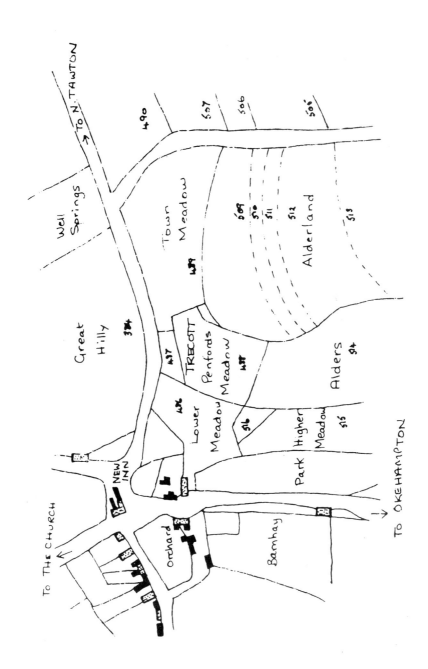

Map of Sandford Courtenay – drawn from the 1840 Tithe Map

Maps reproduced with kind permission of the Diocesan Registrar and the Devon Records Office, Exeter

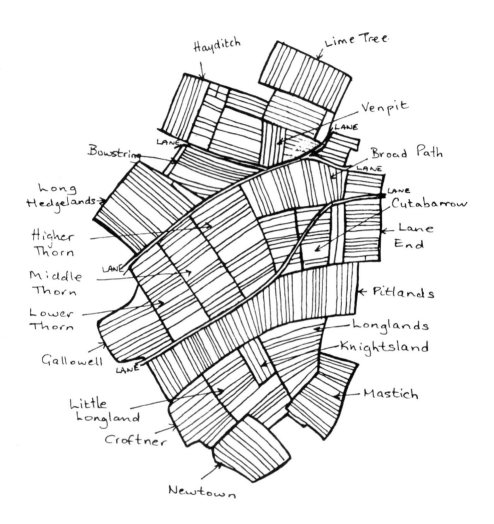

Braunton Great Field, Devon, showing fields with their individual strips

were enclosed by hedges or fences in the seventeenth century. In some places, like Devon however, the process of enclosing fields seems to have begun much earlier, in the twelfth century, and they have the appropriate seven species to confirm this seven hundred years old activity.

Care should be taken, however, as a careful research of written records shows a tradition of deliberately planting five or six species in the eighteenth century. Early enclosure occurs in places where there is sufficient common land and fertile farm land close to settlements.

The field name 'close' is a good indicator of a field hedged because of the Parliamentary Enclosure laws. The last enclosure act was passed in 1903, and a comparison of modern maps with early ones show that very few hedges have been built since the early nineteenth century.

The change from strip farming was necessary for various economic factors, including rising urban populations with the industrial revolution and the growing number of imports, like cotton, which affected the traditional sheep and woollen industry. Yet more efficient methods of farming were needed and came with machines, like the first tractors and threshers, which require larger fields to be effective.

It was during these two periods of enclosure that the small wild animals and bird populations associated with hedgerows doubled in numbers, as woods and forests all but disappeared. With the modern up-rooting of hedges we are now losing many of these birds. Song-bird numbers have fallen by up to fifty per cent in the last twenty years.

The purpose of the hedge, as well as species counting, and the shapes of the fields enclosed, can also give a clue to its age. Defensive banks are usually large and remain unploughed, so a hedge would eventually grow. It would be interesting to date the hedge along the top of Offa's Dyke, which is Saxon in date and marks most of the border between Wales and England. Territorial boundaries, such as the Iron Age (if not earlier) tribal border between the tribes of Devon and Somerset, is in places marked by a hedge, and has remained largely the same throughout the Roman, Saxon and Norman Conquests. The hedge, where it exists, is in places huge and obviously of great antiquity, with up to fourteen species in one area studied. The hedge may not have been allowed to grow at the same time that the bank was built, so some care is needed at times. A long continuous hedge boundary which other field divisions come up to but do not cross, is a very good indication of an old hedge.

Deer parks date from the later Middle Ages and, apart from the shape of the bank, as on page 22, can often be identified from field names.

The actual size of the hedgerow, particularly the bank, is important. A very large bank is an indication that the hedge is old. Farmers use hedges to pile up the stones that are ploughed up in the field, so the bank of a hedge gets bigger and bigger through the ages. Where a hedge runs alongside a road or path, people and traffic wear the road down, so the hedge seen from the road is very tall. Some roads become disused but the evidence for its existence may still remain in the shape of a double hedge. These tracks are called 'Green lanes' or 'Hollow ways' and are an interesting study in themselves.

Some medieval roads were quite wide, due to people varying where they walked or rode when the track got muddy, so when tarmacadam was introduced in the last century, only the middle part of the road was covered. So there are now grass verges with the original hedgebanks quite a long way from the road. Sometimes a new hedge has been planted next to the new road, and two hedges can be found, the older one further away from the road. Sometimes this strip of land has been used as a thin field or garden area.

A further way of dating a hedge is where it runs along something which is dateable, such as a Roman road, but, once again, care is needed as the road may have existed before the Romans came, or the hedge may have been planted later, so a bit of common sense is sometimes needed. Comparative dates can be obtained where a hedge is cut through by such a dateable feature as a Roman road. This can be seen on a map and need not involve actually visiting the site, and once again old maps can help.

The Domesday Book and the thirteenth century onwards estate accounts, court rolls and local surveys may be of assistance with place-name evidence

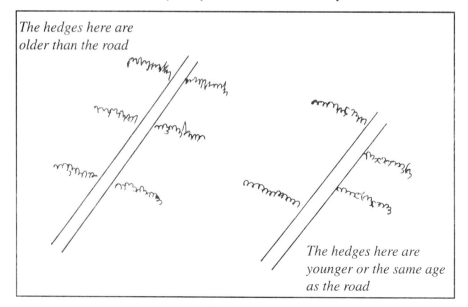

The hedges here are older than the road

The hedges here are younger or the same age as the road

and amounts of woodland, and can be found in Records Offices or the local studies section of the library. Place-names can give clues to possible old hedges, for example 'Old Ditch' and its variations could indicate a very early hedge.

From the sixteenth century, however, we have the first large scale estate maps, giving field and estate boundaries and these are of much more use for hedge dating. They increase in numbers towards the nineteenth century, when most of the country was covered by the Tithe Map series.

There are instances where great care is needed in making judgments about the date of a hedge. Occasionally when a hedge is planted, many species are used to make the hedge look attractive. Beech is a favourite tree for decorative hedges, so if it is found in a hedge, the distances between them should be noted to see if they are usually spaced out in an orderly or deliberate fashion. There is a hedge in Dorset which has thirty species, including many foreign and exotic species, but it is a hedge on a country manor estate, so this hedge was obviously deliberately planted.

Hedgerow dating is now sufficiently established and studied for some minor adjustments to be made. For example, if a hedge is very old and thick, it will be increasingly difficult for new seedlings to establish themselves, so it may take longer than the hundred years given in the formula. This would mean that very old hedges, say over ten species, are even older than the count would suggest. (It would still make them Saxon, which is the most important thing for our kind of study!)

Species differ in other parts of the country, as the soils and climate differ, but the theory still remains the same. There appears to be a maximum number, because there can only be a certain number, about thirteen or fourteen, that like the same soil. However there is a hedge in Dyfed, Wales which has twenty-one species in one hundred and twenty metres, and is the only hedge to be declared a Site of Special Scientific Interest.

Remnant woodland hedges may have many trees in the hedge. Remnant hedges are made when a farmer cuts down a woodland to make a field, leaving some of the woodland trees to form a hedge. Some of these would be cut or coppiced, but would readily sprout again, forming a thick hedge. Oak, Ash, Yew, Sycamore, Lime, Alder, Hazel, Birch, Willow and Sweet Chestnut all respond naturally to coppicing. There would be many different trees in the hedge, but the field and hedge itself would be very new.

Some flowers which grow in woods give us an indication that the hedge used to be part of a wood. These plants are Primrose, Bluebell, Dogs Mercury and Wood Anemone. Some of these grow anywhere, but when you see all four of them together in a hedge, then it is probable that it was once a wood.

INDICATOR HEDGEROW PLANTS

All plants and trees for identification taken from
The Concise British Flora by W. Keble Martin. (Ebury Press) 1965

WOOD ANENOME
Anenome nemorosa
White flower
Indicates former woodland if found in large numbers

PRIMROSE
Primula vulgaris
Pale lemon
Indicates former woodland if found in large numbers

DOGS MERCURY
Mercurialis perennis
Small cream flowers
Indicates former woodland and ancient hedge
if found in large numbers

BLUEBELL
Endymion non-scriptus
Blue flowers
Indicates former woodland and
ancient hedge when found in
large numbers

YELLOW ARCHANGEL
Lamiastrum galeobdolon
Yellow flowers
Indicates ancient hedge when found in large numbers

Another recent study looked at the problem of overgrown hedges. It seems that a badly neglected hedge will lose some of the species. This has implications for hedge dating if you consider the time of the Black Death in England, in the fourteenth century, when an estimated one third of the population died. It is obvious that with the loss of manpower, hedges would have been neglected, and become overgrown, losing some of the species previously established there. The dating of hedges has received a lot of attention from modern studies of various particular aspects, and all have proved the validity of the method, but point out that any errors that occur will show the hedge is younger than it really is, so this is worth bearing in mind. There are some areas of Britain, especially the North and West where stone walls dominate the landscape. It is possible to get a date for these, according to the shape of the field enclosed, but there may be scope for other dating techniques, perhaps by using styles of wall building, or from the flora or insects living on the walls.

DATING USING BRAMBLE

Where there are few species, or where the field boundaries are stone walls, particularly in the West and North of England, there are simply not enough kinds of shrub according to Dr Hooper's criteria to permit the rule to operate. Recent studies of the few species that do grow in these areas have shown that Brambles or Blackberries are amenable to dating.

There are hundreds, if not thousands of true breeding lines of Brambles, each with their own local or regional distribution – three hundred and eighty-seven have been positively identified.

Most hedges have three or four different types of Bramble, but some have as many as eight or nine. It was shown that those hedges were old, either prehistoric routes or, using documentary evidence, were shown to be medieval in date.

The differences between the species are slight, but a book titled *Rubi of Great Britain and Ireland* by W.C.R. Watson (Cambridge 1958) shows all the known species and how to identify them.

In wetland areas such as the Somerset Levels, field boundaries are marked by pollarded willow trees, visible even when the fields are flooded, which happens often. The dating of these boundary trees would have to be done by tree-ring dating. This involves counting the growth rings of the trunks. This technique can be performed on any hedgerow tree after it is felled. One growth ring is added every year, so by a simple process of counting the number of tree rings, the age of the tree can be found.

VARIOUS WAYS OF HEDGE MAKING

NATURALLY GROWING

Stones removed from field and piled around the edges where small trees and shrubs seed themselves.

ACCIDENTALLY

Cut fence posts of some woods can sprout and grow. Hawthorn and hazel do this very easily and were used to make the hurdle fences commomly used in the past.

DELIBERATELY LEFT (REMNANT HEDGE)

Fields created from woodland will have some of the trees from the wood in the hedges. Many Saxon place names like 'leigh' and 'hurst' mean a clearing or settlement in woodland.

DELIBERATELY PLANTED

Hawthorn was the most common tree used for hedging; in fact the name means 'hedge-thorn'. It grows very quickly and has sharp thorns so soon becomes an inpenetrable barrier and provides shelter for the saplings of other species to grow and eventually form a thick hedge. A stockade of animal-proof cut thorn bushes placed on the ground will also sprout and take root, forming a hedge. Ash, beech, elm and sycamore were later popular trees for deliberate planting as hedges.

LAID HEDGES

WELSH LAID HEDGE

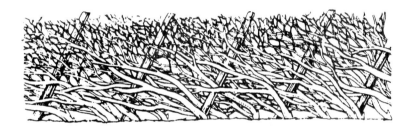

Hedges are 'laid' or woven and tied together to provide extra thicknes and solid growth. In Wales these can still be seen, keeping sheep securely in fields.

MIDLANDS LAID HEDGE

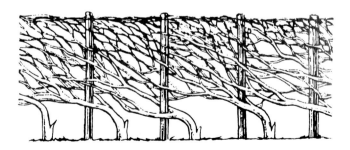

These are designed more for keeping in cattle, so the strength and thickness is needed higher. These hedges need re-laying every few years to prevent them getting too straggly.

SPECIALISED HEDGES AND BANKS

Occasionally something more secure than a simple hedge was needed. The arrangements of the banks and ditches can sometimes tell us about a hedge and why it was planted.

DEER PARKS

Deer can leap into the park quite easily, but cannot get out again as it is easier for deer to leap down than up. These banks are called Deer Leaps. The ditch is usually seven feet wide and the bank, although not high, up to about five feet, is about ten to fifteen feet wide. Deer parks were granted by license so there may be a written record of the foundation of the park, which are normally medieval in date.

Deer can leap into park easily...

Deer Park

...but cannot leap out again

USE THE CENTRE PAGE FOR SPECIES COUNTING

**IT MAY BE PHOTOCOPIED
FOR USE IN THE FIELD.**

*Please note that Dog Rose is counted but
Bramble or Honeysuckle etc., are not.*

WORK SHEET FOR SPECIES COUNTING

LOCATION OF HEDGE and LENGTH WALKED including map reference:

_____

_____

DESCRIPTION OF HEDGE including SIZE, TYPE OF DITCH:

_____

_____

_____

WOODY SPECIES *(circle predominant species if any)*:

LENGTH WALKED	1	2	3	4	5	6

(in multiples of 30 metres)

Alder ....   _____

Ash ....   _____

Aspen ....   _____

Beech ....   _____

Birch ....   _____

Blackthorn ....   _____

Buckthorn ....   _____

Cherry ....   _____

Crab Apple ....   _____

Dog Rose ....   _____

Dogwood ....   _____

Elder ....   _____

Elm ....   _____

Guelder Rose ...   _____

Hawthorn ....   _____

Hazel ....   _____

Holly ....   _____

Hornbeam ....   _____

Maple ....   _____

Oak ....   _____

Privet ....   _____

Rowan ....   _____

Spindle ....   _____

Sycamore ....   _____

Willow ....   _____

Yew ....   _____

OTHERS ....   _____

(Also note how far apart trees are _____)

PLANTS INDICATING FORMER WOODLAND OR AGE
(Circle if abundant)

Primrose   Wood Anenome

Dogs Mercury   Bluebell   Yellow Archangel

CONCLUSIONS ABOUT THE AGE AND HISTORY OF THIS HEDGE:

_____

No. of Species _____

Date of Hedge _____

Adjoining Hedgerows _____

Pattern of Fields _____

_____

_____

_____

_____

_____

_____

_____

_____

_____

_____

_____

_____

_____

_____

_____

_____

_____

_____

_____

_____

_____

_____

_____

_____

_____

IF YOU CANNOT IDENTIFY EACH INDIVIDUAL SPECIES,
IT IS SUFFICIENT TO COUNT THE DIFFERENT
TYPES OF LEAVES.

CARE MUST BE TAKEN NOT TO MISTAKE IMMATURE
OR OLD LEAVES.

ORNAMENTAL HEDGES

Ornamental hedges became popular in Tudor times, following Italian fashion. Many of these ornamental hedges are of evergreen trees, like box or privet. Occasionally finding these in a hedge can indicate a former garden, and possibly a house site. Flowering species were and still are used for ornamental hedges, including trees such as Laburnum. Many hedges will have numerous species, but as these trees are mainly foreign imports are easily distinguished from a basic old indigenous hedge.

Topiary, or the art of trimming or shaping hedges into shapes is still a popular pastime but needs skill and a lot of patience.

DEFENSIVE

Defensive or old territorial boundaries are usually large and have 'v'-shaped ditches. They may still be called dykes like Offa's Dyke or the Wansdyke near Bath.

PACK HORSE ROUTES

Hedge banks sometimes have a step on the side. These have been deliberately cut to allow pack horse loads to pass on narrow lanes.

ALDER
Alnus glutinosa
Common, especially near streams.

A variation may be the Berry-Bearing Alder (*frungula alnus*) which has black berries. Also called Black Alder it was once used as a tooth cleaner and for skin conditions. The Common Alder was recommended for sore feet and for getting rid of fleas. Alder is poisonous and used to produce a yellow or green dye.

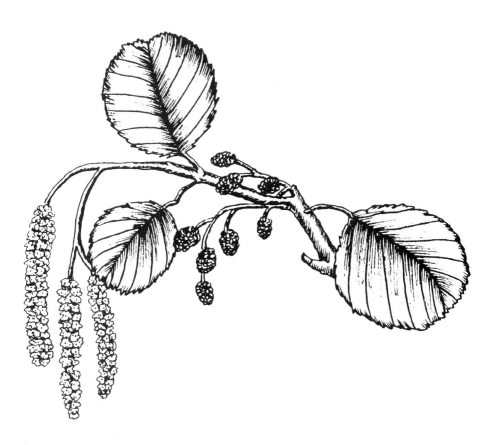

ASH
Fraxinus excelsior
Identifiable from its black leaf buds. Ash is a suitable wood for handles for tools because it withstands shock well. It was used in prehistoric times for spear shafts and later small farm implements and household objects. Today it is used for hockey sticks, billiard cues and oars. Ash is good for building, as it is a hard, durable wood. It is poisonous to cattle, affecting their stomachs. A pale yellow dye was obtained from the bark, which, when burnt was used as a medication for leprous or scabby heads, and was alleged to protect against adder bites.

ASPEN, or Trembling Poplar
Populus tremula
Common, especially on wet ground. It is a very hard wood, suitable for building and will endure as long as oak, although it is not so popular.

BEECH
Fagus sylvatica
Common but tends to prefer chalky soils. Beech wood has no smell or taste, so is used for children's toys and kitchen utensils. The nuts were valuable fodder, especially for pigs. Beech nuts, apart from being edible, make a useful vegetable oil, and the leaves can be distilled to make a liquor.

BIRCH (SILVER)
Betula pendula
Common. The white bark with black diamond shapes has been extensively used throughout history. The Ice Man, whose 5,000 year-old body was found frozen in the Alps, had with him a container made of birch bark, in which he carried his equipment for making fire. If he had got a headache or other pain, he could have chewed his container, for the bark contains aspirin, and was extensively used as a medicine throughout the ages and was especially effective against rheumatism. Birch bark also produces yellow, brown and purple dyes.

BLACKTHORN (SLOE)
Prunus spinosa
Sloe berries have been used to make gin since the Iron Age, about 1,000BC and to make blue and brown colourings. Similar to the Blackthorn, but having no thorns and oblong fruit, is the WILD PLUM (*Prunus domestica*) which is found in the Midlands and Eastern England. It is edible, usually as jams or jellies.

The BULLACE
Prunus domestica insititia
or Wild Damson is another of this family commonly found in hedges. It also has no thorns, but has round fruit. Damsons also provide a purple dye.

BUCKTHORN
Rhamnus catharticus
Common in Midlands and South-East England. Buckthorn is the source of blue and green dyes.

CHERRY (GEAN)
Prunus avium
There may be other trees which are not wild, but which have escaped from orchards. In the North and Midlands fruit trees were deliberately planted in hedges. Cherry wood is red-brown or deep red and was used for fine furniture, tobacco pipes and musical instruments.

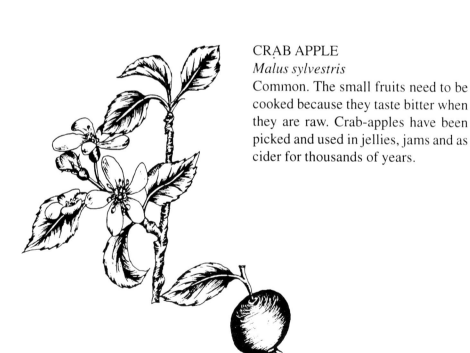

CRAB APPLE
Malus sylvestris
Common. The small fruits need to be cooked because they taste bitter when they are raw. Crab-apples have been picked and used in jellies, jams and as cider for thousands of years.

DOGROSE
Rosa canina
Common. There are many species of
wild rose but only one per hedge is
counted. The Dog Rose is one of the
most interesting and useful plants
found in a hedge. Various foods and
drinks, as well as medicines are made
from the dog rose. Today it is drunk as
a tea and as a general health remedy
but in the past all the different parts of
the plant had their medicinal uses.
Rose Hips are an excellent source of
vitamin C, usually as Rose Hip Syrup.

DOGWOOD
Swida sanduinea
Common on chalk soils, especially in
Southern England – rare in the North,
Scotland and Wales. Dogwood will
only grow if there are already at least,
four species well established, so if you
see it in a hedge you can conclude it is
over four hundred years old.

ELDER
Sambucus nigra
Common, except in Northern Scotland.
Elder is useful for three dyes: green,
black and purple. Elderberries make
sauces, jam and drinks but it can be
poisonous in large quantities. Elder
was a useful addition to the medicine
cupboard, both in the past and now. The
flowers, bark, leaves and berries were
and are used for the complexion, as a
source of vitamin C, as a diuretic and
for bruises.

ELM
Ulmus procera
There are many species of elm,
including the common hedgerow elm,
the WYCH ELM (*Ulmus Glabra*). All
elms are sadly rarer now following
Dutch Elm disease but were in the past
used as a cure for baldness. Elm is
resistant to water, so was used for
making waterwheels, coffins and
dockyards as well as ships. It is a very
good building material and will last for
hundreds of years. Elm suckers were
used for making wattle or hurdles as
they are pliable enough to be woven
together.

GUELDER ROSE
Vibernum Opulus
Common, but prefers damp areas. May also be known by its country name of 'Mayball'. Occasionally used to make sauces and drinks.

HAWTHORN
Crataegus monogyna
Most common of all hedgerow species, it is also known by its country name 'Bread and Cheese'. There is another species, the MIDLAND HAWTHORN, otherwise called the TWO-STYLED HAWTHORN (*Crataegus laevigata*) which is only found in the Midlands and Southern England. Its leaves are broader than the common hawthorn and the flowers have two styles. Both species may be found in the same hedge and produce hybrids. Sauces and drinks can be made from the berries, and the leaves can be used as salad vegetables. The flowers can also be made into a liquor. Hawthorn is a modern medicinal aid to the circulation, but the whole plant was used for all kinds of medicinal purposes.

— Anther

— Style

— Ovary

MIDLAND
HAWTHORN

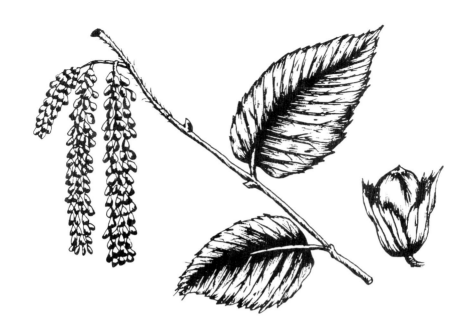

HAZEL
Coryllus avellana

Common, bearing catkins in early spring and nuts in the autumn. Hazel nuts are very high in protein and have been found in baskets collected by Neolithic man, thousands of years ago. They were also used medicinally to cure coughs.

Hazel in abundance is a sign that the hedge is ancient. It sprouts easily and is often used as one of the first plants to make a hedge. Hazel twigs are pliable enough to he woven together for making wattle or hurdles, so may have been deliberately planted for local industries. It is often common on the edges of woods, so may be a clue to a remnant woodland hedge. Hazel wood and twigs were and are used for making fishing rods, whip handles, barrel hoops, walking sticks, thatch ties and water-divining rods. When burnt, the charcoal was used for gunpowder.

HOLLY
Ilex aquifolium
Common evergreen. The berries are poisonous, but the leaves were used as winter fodder for cattle. Holly branches were once thought to protect houses from lightning and men from witchcraft. It was thought to be unlucky to cut one as it was the favourite tree of the fairies. The sharp pointed leaves were made into a fomentation for broken bones. A bundle of holly twigs were once used to sweep chimneys, and the wood, which is the densest of our native hardwoods, was used for carving, inlaying and woodcuts. Pianos, mathematical instruments, knife handles and coffins were all made from holly.

HORNBEAM
Carpinus betulus
Common in the South-East but found all over England, although it is rare in Wales and Scotland. It is a very tough hard wood, and reputed to be as tough as horn but it is not flexible and consequently little used in carpentry. In former times, its principal use was for the actions in pianos, cogs and wooden screws.

MAPLE
Acer campestre
Common from Yorkshire southwards, rare to the North. If you see Field Maple in a hedge you can conclude it is over four hundred years old, as it will only grow if there are already at least four species well established.

OAK
Quercus robur
Pedunculate oak is gnarled and sprawling. It is common, and often found as pollarded trees.

SESSILE OAK
Quercus petreaea
This is taller than the Pedunculate and more common in the North and West of the country, also common on acid soils. The acorns and leaves are poisonous, and make brown coloured dyes,but can also be used as an astringent and skin cleanser. Oak was used in buildings, as it does not rot in the ground and can readily be split into planks. In Neolithic times when the first houses were built, ancient thick Oak forests covered the countryside. Oak trees were planted every twenty-two yards, at the end of the strips of the Medieval Open Field farming system.

PRIVET
Ligustrum vulgare
Common in Southern England, but often used as an ornamental decorative hedge. Dyes of yellow and green are obtained from Privet, but the berries are harmful if eaten.

ROWAN (MOUNTAIN ASH)
Sorbus aucuparia
Common in North and West, but also found elsewhere. Rowan berries make sauces and drinks, but was, and is, planted in Scotland where there is a superstition it conveys health and wealth to the household. The wood is used for the handles of tools and bows.

SPINDLE

Euonymus europaeus

Common in Southern England but extends to Southern Scotland, it got its name from its use in making the hand spindles used for spinning wool. It is a very hard wood, useful for knitting needles, skewers, pegs, etc. Spindle berries, the bark and leaves are all poisonous. A hedge will have to be six hundred years old before Spindle can grow in it, as it needs thick shelter for its seedlings.

SYCAMORE

Acer pseudoplanatanus

Common everywhere. Sycamore were popular in the eighteenth century and deliberately planted for their appearance. It is a favourite wood for musical instruments, especially harps.

WILLOW (COMMON SALLOW)
Salix atrocinerea

There are many species of willow: the shapes of the leaves and flowers vary in different parts of the country. Common in wetland areas such as the Somerset Levels, where the field boundaries are marked by pollarded willow trees and are used for making hurdles, baskets and cricket bats, as well as providing a yellow dye. The wood is also used for making musical instruments and artificial limbs. Aspirin is found in willow bark, so was used in the past as a medicine to relieve pain and inflamation, while the leaves were used to clear dandruff.

YEW
Taxus baccata

Usually found on limestone and chalk, but as it is highly poisonous to livestock it is rare in hedges, usually only found around churchyards, where it was planted to prevent plague. The wood is dense and elastic and was in the past used to make long-bows, spears and dagger handles.

HEDGEROW USES

WOOD

All woods had their own special uses, either because of the particular qualities of each wood or from tradition. These uses have been detailed in the summaries of the diagrams of the trees and shrubs.

Hedges were also a very, important source of firewood, especially for the poor.

FOOD AND DRINK

Fungi

A thick old hedge is a perfect environment for fungi, as it provides a deep plant litter with little light. Common hedgerow fungi today are Parasol mushrooms, Shaggy Cap and Giant Puffball but, as always, with fungi great care must be taken with identification. Historically there were more fungi than today with up to three hundred edible species, many of which grew in hedges.

Nuts

Hazel is a very common hedgerow tree. Hazel nuts are very nutritious, containing fifty per cent more protein than eggs. A fifteenth century cookbook also uses the leaves of the Hazel in a recipe. The Romans introduced many plants and trees to this country, including the Sweet Chestnut. Although these are trees of parkland and woodland, they do sometimes seed in hedges. Beech nuts, apart from being edible, make a useful vegetable oil, and the leaves can be distilled to make a liquor similar to gin.

Acorns are bitter to the taste but have, in the past, been ground to make flour. When roasted twice, acorns make a coffee substitute. Walnuts were bought to this country between four and five hundred years ago, but the trees are increasingly rare, as the wood was very popular.

Fruits

Blackberry picking is a late summer occupation for thousands of children (and adults) and has been enjoyed since prehistoric times. It is a clear indication that some species in a hedgerow are edible, but it is surprising just how many have been eaten by man. Hedges must have, over the years, provided a very valuable food source to all kinds of peoples in the past. Raspberries are fruits of the forest originally but also grow in hedgerows and are traditionally popular in Scotland. Strawberries, wild cherries, pear, red and blackcurrants and gooseberries are all found in hedges, although increasingly less so.

Rowan, Guelder Rose and Elderberries make very nice sauces and drinks, while Sloe has provided the basis of gin since the Iron Age. Rose Hips are an excellent source of vitamin C and were collected by schoolchildren during and after the second world war for the manufacture of Rose Hip Syrup.

Leaves

Dandelions are useful hedgerow food and drink plants, providing wine and a salad green from the leaves, and a coffee substitute from the roots. The root of Lords and Ladies was used in making salop, a traditional sweet dish like tapioca. The leaves of lime trees, strawberries, hawthorn and yarrow can all be used as salad vegetables. Fat Hen (or Good King Henry) has leaves with more iron and protein than cabbage or spinach. It has been found in the stomach of the mummified bodies dating to the Iron Age buried in peat bogs. Also with long histories are Hogweed, Hops, Yellow Archangel, Common Mallow, and Ground Elder, which was a Roman introduction and used, as were the others, as vegetables.

Samuel Pepys and Sir Walter Scott both praised Stinging Nettles, using them for soup, porridge, as a vegetable (rich in iron), a herbal tea and for beer. These were yet another Roman introduction, as were Alexanders and Burdock, the stems of which were both used as pot herbs. Other flavourings include Ransoms, a strong garlic flavour, and Meadowsweet, Cow Parsley and Woodruff.

Goosegrass is an edible green vegetable and the seeds can be used to make coffee, but the seeds were also used for the tops of lacemakers pins, and the stems and leaves made a very good strainer.

Flowers

The Dog Rose is one of the most interesting plants found in a hedge. The petals were, and still are, used for celebrations, and there is a record of a Roman banquet where so many were scattered that some of the guests suffocated! They were also used to make rosaries (hence the name) for the Roman Catholic Church. More prosaic uses for the petals, include wine, tea, brandy, vinegar, honey, candy, Turkish delight, jelly and crystalised fruits and, with rhubarb, a very nice jam.

Another fine jam is Elderflower and Gooseberry. Violets, Primroses and Cowslips used to be made into crystalised sweets. The flowers of Hawthorn and Lime were made into a liquor and mild sedative tea respectively. The flowers of Hops are considered essential for brewing, but in the past Ground Ivy was used to flavour and clarify the ale.

MEDICINES

It is interesting to compare a modern herbal remedies book with one on traditional country cures, and the most familiar old book on herbs is Nicholas Culpeper's *Herbal*, written in the early seventeenth century. Many of the remedies they mention are obtained from hedges, Culpeper in fact wrote his book specifically so that ordinary people could gather wild herbal medicines from hedgerows instead of paying inflated apothecaries' prices. He was not popular with that profession, needless to say.

It is highly likely that farm animals, like cows, make use of the medicinal properties of some hedgerow plants. A farmer today says he keeps his vet's bills down by allowing areas of uncut hedge and verge for the cows to graze.

Some remedies are pure superstition, such as the practice of planting a hedge of Box around the house to prevent plague. The planting of Yew hedges around churchyards was for similar reasons. Pliny suggested that Holm (Holly) branches protected houses from lightning and men from witchcraft! Other remedies have been found to have a sound basis. Most obvious is the use of Foxglove leaves. They are poisonous, unless you have a heart condition, in which case certain doses of digitalis are a very effective medicine, in use today under the trade name of digoxin. Culpeper also said it was a cure for scabby head, but it is uncertain if this aspect has been tested.

Aspirin is today manufactured from chemicals, but it is the exact same chemicals found in willow bark. Culpeper also suggests the leaves will clear dandruff. Aspirin is also found in Primrose leaves, which Culpeper used as a salve for wounds, and Birch bark, also used today as an anti-rheumatic.

Both modern herbalists and Culpeper agree that stinging nettles are good for arthritis, gout and joint pains. Nettle tea was traditionally drunk to clean the blood and to cure eczema and goitre. Elder or 'God's Stinking Tree' is also universally accepted as a useful addition to the medicine cupboard, both in the past and now. The flowers, bark, leaves and berries were and are used for the complexion, as a diuretic, for bruises and inflammations, and as a source of vitamin C against colds respectively. Raspberry leaves and fruit are also generally acknowledged to be useful for constipation and every child knows dandelions are a diuretic.

The single most important plant, however, is the rose. Today it is drunk as a tea as a general health remedy but in the past Culpeper reckoned it cured or helped just about everything. All the different parts of the plant had their uses, including 'a certain white worm found in the hips which is used to expel worms from the body'.

Some remedies have a very long history, for example it is recorded that the Romans used to plant Mugwort or Wormwood in hedgerows for travellers to ease their aching feet. Some plants are still recommended today. These include Oak (an astringent and skin cleanser), Bryony (a modern Anti-rheumatic and in past times used to clear 'Running cankers, gangrenes and tetters'), Honeysuckle (for asthma and coughs both past and present), Broom (a diuretic and cure for headlice), Hawthorn (a modern aid to the circulation from the flowers and the seeds and in Culpeper's time for 'inward tormenting pains') and Hops (for insomnia).

Woodcut from the title-page of the fourth edition of the 'Grete Herball' (1561)

Some modern remedies were not recorded by Culpeper, including Broom and Lily of the Valley, both mild diuretics, and Barberry, an antiseptic. Violets are good for skin conditions and are currently being studied for anti-cancer treatment. The list from Culpeper, however, gives an idea of how valuable hedgerows were for people before chemical medicines. They include Black Alder (used to clean teeth but also cure the itch and scabs), Common Alder (eases sore feet and clears a room of fleas), Yellow Archangel (for sores, tumours and women's conditions), Ash (The burnt bark helps against leprous or scabby heads, and protects against vipers), Beechnuts (good for hot swellings), Blackberry (clears up putrid sores of the mouth and secret parts), Cherries (helps expel wind), Elm (a cure for baldness), Hazel nuts (with mead and pepper helps an old cough), Holly (a fomentation for broken bones), Ivy (for scalds and burns) and, last but not least, Dogs Mercury (cures deafness, catarrh, tetters, ringworms and the itch).

It is evident from the above that some of the treatments are highly suspect, but even more so when one considers that some of the plants are poisonous.

POISONS

Many poisonous plants are now used in mainstream medicine as well as in alternative therapies. Broom, for example was used for women's ailments and gave its name to the witches' broom, but it is poisonous, as are the medicinal plants Dogs Mercury, Oak (acorns and leaves), Ash (which also affects the rumen in cattle), Foxgloves, Elder, Lily of the Valley, Alder and Black Bryony. White Bryony is also poisonous, even the roots, if left in the ground, can poison cattle. It is also addictive, like some other poisonous species which animals and children can be tempted to try, like Buttercups, Laurel, Rhododendrons, Rushes, Horse Radish and Woody Nightshade.

Other hedgerow plants are poisonous, some only slightly, like Daffodils, Snowdrops and Bluebells, Box, Ivy and Mistletoe but others are very dangerous either to people or animals. Yew, as previously mentioned, is very dangerous, even lethal, which accounts for its rarity in hedges. All parts of the Laburnum are also highly toxic, and the Deadly Nightshade is also aptly named, it produces scopalomine, the famous truth drug from James Bond and other films. Cuckoo Pint or 'Parson in the Pulpit' has berries which are deadly, but its leaves were used for starch. Bracken is a severe purgative which can kill, and the berries of Privet and Travellers Joy or Old Mans Beard are also harmful. Spindle berries can be injurious, as well as the bark and leaves.

St John's Wort is used by people as a treatment for depression, but is poisonous for animals. Ragwort is so dangerous to animals it is listed by the Mnistry of Agriculture as an injurious weed, and they can prosecute if it is not removed when found. In spite of their toxicity some of these species were and still are planted because of their usefulness in other ways. Soapwort (Hedge Pink), for example, was gathered and the stems and leaves soaked and boiled to be used as a soap for washing.

DYES

Until the development of chemical dyes this century, the only ways of obtaining dyes was from nature. These included earth pigments, animals (like insects) and most importantly plants. Many hedgerow species were used, providing earthy shades: yellows, greens and browns in the main. All parts of the plants were tried, some plants were useful for their leaves, others for their roots, berries, bark or flowers.

Some species provide more than one colour, for example Birch bark, which makes yellow, brown and purple, and Blackberries make blue, red, black and brown. Elder is useful for three hues, green, black and purple, while many other hedge plants provide two colours, like yellow and green from Privet and Bracken. Dogs Mercury supplies yellow and blue; Sloe provides blue and brown; Buckthorn blue and green. Alder yellow and green and St John's Wort provides red and yellow. Yellow was also obtained from Ash, Broom, Pear, Plum, Poplar, Willow and Barberry. Whortleberries made a good blue, while Bryony and Damson yielded a purple tone. Hops, Larch, Oak, Pine cones and Walnut make various different brown coloured dyes. A red dye was made from Dandelions and Lily of the Valley made a shade of green, but most important are Nettles. Stinging Nettles were collected in tons during the second world war and the dye was used for camouflage nets. Nettles are also fibrous and can be woven into a cloth.

ANIMALS

Hedges and their banks are home to many animals, some of which were useful to man. The hedgehog was evidently named from its hedge home and was, like rabbits, a food. Badgers and foxes use hedgebanks for their homes, and there was a bounty paid for every fox or badger killed, which must have helped some poor folk in a country parish.

Hedges were built to certain specifications for the conservation of game birds, which were also a source of food. Hundreds of birds build their nests in hedges and, in the Middle Ages these nests were eaten, as were the birds themselves. Hedges are important for birds, as they are rich in insect life, buds, seeds, fruits and berries. Blackbird, Thrush, Fieldfare and Redwing particularly appreciate the fact that hedges are richer in food than woodland. Chaffinch and sparrow are the most numerous, averaging one breeding pair every hundred metres, a total countrywide of ten million. Other animals are of no immediate use to man but have their role in the ecological chain. They include mice, common and pigmy shrews, voles, weasels, and stoats. Amphibians and reptiles include lizards and snakes, and especially if there is a wet ditch, frogs and toads.

THE DESTRUCTION OF HEDGES AND THE FUTURE

Although hedges have changed through time because of different practices and inventions such as larger ox teams and heavier ploughs, the greatest damage to hedges has been done during the last fifty years. Recent studies have shown that ten thousand miles of hedge has been ripped out every ten years. In spite of this, they still cover an area equal to one third of the area of deciduous woodland in this country. Many of the hedges surrounding small fields, like the prehistoric and the Saxon fields, have been ripped out by modern farmers as large fields are easier to farm with machinery. The use of chemical sprays has also harmed some of the hedgerow plants, and the mechanised cutting of hedges, which chops the plants and trees in straight lines, also damages many delicate species, making the hedges straggly and thin in places. Before machine cutting, hedges were pruned and cut carefully to ensure they remained thick and bushy.

Even so, there are still plenty of hedges which, when you look at the countryside, are the oldest things you can see, older than the oldest buildings, churches or castles. Only Roman and prehistoric remains, which are quite rare, are older than many common hedges in Britain.

More work is currently being undertaken to examine hedges, not only from an environmental point of view, but also from a historical perspective. There is a small study which suggests that dating can also be done from the snail population. There is scope for investigating the insect population to see if they can provide dating techniques which may be more precise than tree species.

If it were possible to date EVERY hedge in the country, we should have a great map through time, showing how the beautiful countryside of this country came to look as it does.

In places where the greatest loss of hedges has occurred, like East Anglia, the rate of destruction has declined as ecological factors, such as wind erosion, have been affecting crops. The rate of decline of hedges has decreased since its peak in the 1960s but the countryside and hedgerows are still under threat from development. I hope this little book will increase interest and awareness of the great importance of hedges in historical studies and aid the campaign to minimise their destruction.

SPECIES INDEX

GENERAL INDEX

FURTHER READING

These books are easily obtained and anyone interested in the countryside and its history will find them invaluable.

The Making of the English Landscape
W.G. Hoskins (Penguin) 1970.

Discovering Hedgerows
D. Streeter & R. Richards (BBC) 1982

Hedges
E. Pollard, M.D. Hooper & N.W. Moore (Collins) 1974.

Trees and Woodlands in the British Landscape
O. Rackham (Dent) 1981.

ORCHARD PUBLICATIONS: SIMILAR READING

The Birds and Natural History of the South Hams
by Gordon Waterhouse

Wildlife of the Salcombe and Kingsbridge Estuaries
by Gordon Waterhouse

A Dartmoor Naturalist – Woodlands
by Tony Hills